Table of Contents

INTRODUCTION: Who is this Book for?

In my 5 years of experience as a Tech business Expert, I have noticed that there are two types of Business owners; those who are oblivious to the role of Technology in the growth of their business (people who are very comfortable with the progress of their business that they don't see technology as a necessary tool). The second group are those who believe technology is vital for their business. They are curious and are continuously trying tools and looking for effective ways that will grow their business using technology. If you are in the second category, I am glad to tell you: **This book is meant for you.**

Until the COVID Lockdown in 2020, a lot of businesses in Nigeria did not think that "Technology in Business" was a must-have and many businesses without online presence suffered

huge financial losses. However, while we can all

agree that technology is a great tool, we must also

understand that it is not a Magic Wand. You have

to put in the work if you want to get good results.

In this book, I will introduce you to tools that will

help you stand out from your competition. You will

also be introduced to practical steps that I have

used personally to increase business sales online

and I will guide you to try them out in your

business. It going to be Money & Fun!!!

Why should you adhere to the information I have written in this Book?

When I started building a Brand, one of my biggest mistakes was thinking that simply creating a website and social media accounts was enough to run my business online. I understood that these tools were very vital to the growth of my business online, but I was ignorant about how they would.

*I understood that these tools were very vital to the growth of my business online, but I was **ignorant** about how they would.*

Over the years as I worked with clients to build their Brand reputation online and drive sales, I have observed that "HOW" you present your business online is very key to the success of that business. I discovered a lot of business owners treat Technology as an "Asset" and not as a "Tool". A great number of Clients contact our company to develop websites and apps merely because it is a must-have asset for any reputable business online (not necessarily with a commitment to drive more sales with those tools). This is not healthy for any business.

Having made a couple of mistakes & experimenting, I have seen a handful of practical strategies that work and strategies that don't. For instance, in November 2020, I moved from 0 sales online in my first week to generating over 400,000 over a 3 weeks period (online sales). Nnitiwe Tech Limited (My company) has worked with Private & Federal Government Organizations (*Universities, Churches, Companies…*) as well as Individuals (*Coaches, Small Business Owners, Music Artists…*). I have helped some of these organizations to cut down the cost of advertising by up to 90% (in some cases) and increased sales and engagements by up to 50%.

I have helped businesses move beyond;

- Number of Likes
- Number of views
- Number of visits

- Number of Post comments
- Number of Followers

I have helped business owners to convert these metrics to the number of Sales. I have applied these same results to my company and have seen results and I have decided to share key strategies with you so that you do business online the right way.

Challenges Addressed in this Book

This book addresses the challenges faced by Entrepreneurs running businesses online. This book is not ideal for an any one who is trying to figure out what type of business/product & services to run/ sell.

This book will give you clarity and serve as a practical guide on the best practices when setting up a **NEW BUSINESS** online or improving **EXISTING BUSINESS** already running online.

CHAPTER 1 - Business Review: Is my idea sellable?

Thousands of Business ideas hit the market every day and many of these concepts look and sound great but only a handful pass the test. When we try to test business concepts to find the reasons some businesses are not successful; conclusions for some will point us to a crappy business idea while some will be linked with faults in business structure & processes (This subject is beyond the scope of this book).

The good news is that there are ways to find out if your products, services, and business processes/structure will sell. We will briefly look at them in the next section of this chapter.

Running a Business that fills a need

In order to run a successful business, your idea needs to:

1. Solve a problem

2. Be sellable (something people will be willing to pay for).
3. Generate Profit!

As funny as it sounds, some Entrepreneurs are running successful charity organizations because they are missing a key ingredient, Profit! This is because selling is not synonymous with profit generation.

---

*Some Entrepreneurs are running successful **charity organizations** because they are missing a key ingredient, **PROFIT!***

To decide if your business idea is workable, here are some questions you need to find positive answers to:

1. Is the problem you are trying to solve relatable to a common group of people or is it a personal interest? (Market size)

2. Will people be willing to pay for the solution you are offering at the quality and price you are offering?
3. Is it profitable? In the long run, can the business sustain itself?
4. Wear the shoes of the Customer, would you buy from him /her?
5. Who are your Competitors?
6. What makes you a better option for your customers? (in comparison to your Competitors)
7. Who is your Ideal Client? (who needs the solution you are offering).
8. What can you do to stand out and blow the mind of your customers?

Do not be emotionally attached to your Business Idea

Building a successful business requires a lot of energy, commitment, strategy, and patience. Growing a business to become successful requires a lot of effort. This level of dedication can make the Entrepreneur become emotionally attached to that business to a point that blinds them from assessing business decisions & evaluations objectively.

In November 2020 I attended a 6 weeks virtual business training by Steve Harris (a Business Coach) and one of the lessons from that training was the need for business owners to be logical and not too emotionally connected to their business so that they can test their business idea to see if is a profitable one or just **a concept they are in love with**.

CHAPTER 2 - Don't freak out: No Tech god required

Not everybody was born to become a Techie but every Entrepreneur needs to have their business well represented online. I know the mere thought of this scares a lot of you. You probably share these doubts/complaints:

- Tech is too complex;
- I don't want to be a Techie;
- Hiring a Techie is pretty expensive;
- I want to build my website myself. But coding looks like sorcery;

It is really not that complicated (and this is non-techie me speaking 😊). Contrary to popular opinion, once you understand clearly the problem you want technology to solve, you have placed yourself on a path of success.

Don't be unnecessarily sophisticated

You do not have to figure out everything on your own! Many business owners make this mistake. I have had countless cases where Clients come asking me to develop software apps/ features or to execute a project and after careful analysis, it revealed that what they are requesting would not help them meet the goals & targets they have planned and projected.

My advice is, speak to an expert. Get your goals & objectives clear, then talk to a Consultant who will

Great solutions don't have to be sophisticated. The excellence is not in the **Sophistication.**

give you a breakdown of your options (the financial implications, advantage, and disadvantage) from a professional angle. That way, you will be in a better place to make a smarter decision that will lead to massive results.

Also, my philosophy is; great solutions don't have to be sophisticated. The excellence is not in the sophistication.

This means that if after a balanced evaluation you realize a tool can help you solve a problem without having to heavily in building one from scratch, then go for it.

CHAPTER 3 - Build an Online Community

Business is about attention. Your ability to catch the attention of potential customers will put you in a better place to make sales. The main reason why people value reason Web traffic, YouTube views, Post likes and Account followers is because they have a direct correlation with **Attention**. To able sell your products to a complete stranger online, you need to get and keep their attention.

In times past, successful mediums of advertisement have always been those mediums that get the attention of the average potential customer; Newspapers, Radio stations, Billboards, Television,

*Successful **mediums of advertisement** have always been those mediums that get the attention of the average potential customer; Newspapers, Radio stations, Billboards, Television, and in today's world, **THE INTERNET**.*

and in today's world, THE INTERNET. This is why you must consider having a strong presence online because your potential customers are already surfing the net.

An online community is a group of loyal Individuals who feed on your content and are genuinely interested in what you are offering. This group is a pool filled with potential customers who will pay for your services and products if they get a good deal. We will be looking at different ways in which you can grow a community.

Branding: Businesses will be addressed the way they are represented

There is a popular saying: **"You will be addressed how you dress"**, well sorry to break to you but unfortunately it is not limited to just clothes. While the true values and goals of an organization can be visualized/ understood over time, the first impression would decide to a great extent if people will choose to work with your Brand or not.

Branding goes beyond a great-looking logo & a beautiful website. The way you respond to potential Customers, the contents you post online… how you make people feel, that's your Brand. Branding is not what you tell people about your

> *BRANDING is not what you tell people about your business. It is THE EXPERIENCE people remember when they think about your business.*

business. It is the experience people remember when they think about your business.

Building a Brand

The first step to building a great Brand (both Offline and Online) is finding your business identity. You need to understand who your audience is; people who are interested in buying the type of service you are offering. Knowing:

- Their age;
- Location;
- Job Category;

- Gender;
- Interests and Behavior patterns;
- Hobbies (how they spend time online);
- Content that interests them (especially in comparison with your competition).

This information helps to guide you to understand your potential customers and how to capture their attention. It also helps you know which technologies to invest your time more in. For instance, a Fashion Designer & Makeup Artist will need to a lot of time on Instagram while a Copywriter will have to rank the use of LinkedIn over Instagram (this does not make Instagram any less important. It also does not mean that they are to abandon the use of Instagram).

Once you have defined your audience, the next thing you need to do is to analyze your competitors. Find out how your Competitors are delivering their goods, their strengths, weaknesses and how you can excel in a saturated event. You need to STAND OUT to get your customer's attention in a saturated space where there are many business owners offering similar services. There are endless ways in which you can stand out to capture attention:

1. **Choose a brand name that stands out**.
   When you hear the names- Facebook, Nike, Bitcoin, Apple, eBay, they have something in common. They are easy to remember, catchy, and not complex. By choosing a good name, you could stir curiosity in the minds of potential customers which is good for business and a great tagline is perfect icing on the cake. After all:
   Proverbs 22:1a – "**A good name is to be chosen rather than great riches...**" (☺ Just kidding. Not to be quoted out of context).
2. **Create a mind-blowing graphic representation of your business online**.
   This includes but is not limited to having:
   a. Great looking logo that appeals to the brand's goals, values, and audience.
   b. Professional, responsive, easy-to-use website/app.
   c. Brand colors, fonts, and styles.

    d. Video intros, logo reveals & promotional video content.

3. **Engage your audience with entertaining and resourceful content online**. You can choose to capture your user's attention in a number of ways using Social media or Blogging tools:

    a. Creative & engaging posts on social media (Instagram, Twitter, WhatsApp, Facebook Pages, LinkedIn, Tik Tok…).

    b. Use platforms like Blogger, WordPress & Medium to grow a reading audience. Write captivating articles that relate to your brand but also valuable to the reader.

    c. YouTube, Vimeo, and Social Media streaming services can be used to feed the audience with creative video blogging content.

    d. Newsletters. This is sometimes seen as outdated but it can be used smartly to yield amazing results too.

4. **Improve your Customer experience & processes**. You can make things less difficult

for your customers by improving the way you handle the following operations:

a. Online payments & Invoices.
b. Scheduling & holding meetings.
c. Customer support & Project management.
d. Take and deliver Orders.

Quality over Quantity: Sometimes numbers lie

As I earlier mentioned, attention is very valuable for businesses online. So, when Entrepreneurs don't get the high traffic, likes, or amazing engagements they think they deserve, they get very discouraged. This sometimes can make you feel you are getting it all wrong.

Just as the popular saying goes, "Rome was not built in a day". Getting your business goals, structure, and services right does not guarantee automatic/ immediate growth. Unfortunately, sometimes business owners try to trick the system

*Unfortunately, sometimes business owners try to trick the system by getting buying fake likes & engagements (**Robots**).*

by getting buying fake likes & engagements (robots).

These strategies only give weak and temporary results.

Firstly, Tech companies (Google, Facebook…) are aware of these schemes and constantly work to improve algorithms so that fake insights do not win over qualitative content. This means for instance that on Instagram, having a high number of likes is no longer a strong metric for judging how valuable your content is.

Secondly, except you want to sell your services to robots, your content losses its value. If you invest in fake likes, fake followers, you will not be able to identify content that truly attracted potential customers and this means that you will not be able to sell to more people through DM Marketing and follow-up.

Also, sometimes post engagements are ways our friends and family try to express support for the business. This means that not every like, comment, or share can be interpreted as a **genuine interest in business products/services**.

For these reasons, it is important for business owners not to be fooled by numbers. If you are getting high numbers, filter them and find potential customers & just because you are not getting those high numbers doesn't mean the business is not making progress.

Social Media

Your business needs social media because your customers are already there. As a business owner, a social media presence helps you connect with your customers and even understand them better. Sometimes, however, it can be challenging to know the direction to take:

- What to post;
- When to post;
- What platforms to work with; and
- How to win your potential customers over;

Here is something vital to keep in mind, your customers are on social media to have fun and be entertained. You on the other side want to sell. It is very important that you don't irritate your audience with spam content.

*Your customers are on social media to have **FUN** and be entertained. You on the other side want to **SELL**.*

I have decided to talk about some key social platforms, before we get to discuss them, here are some concepts you need to get familiar with.

1. **Hashtags:** is a keyword or phrase preceded by a **hash sign (#),** used on social media

websites and applications, to find & tag content (Social media posts) on a specific topic. Hashtags was introduced by Twitter in 2007 and ever since has been adapted by other social media platforms.

Using Hashtags intelligently in your posts helps you reach a new audience who find the topics used in the hashtags interesting. This is a good way to grow your audience.

2. **Stories**: Social media stories is a feature on social platforms that allows users to share **full-screen, vertical videos and images** that appear outside of your regular feed and only last for 24 hours before they disappear. This feature was first introduced by Snapchat and later got adopted by other social media platforms such as Instagram, Facebook, YouTube, LinkedIn.

   Stories sharing is a creative way of getting your message to potential customers in **30 seconds or less**. A lot of companies are using stories to capture their customers' attention (platforms like Instagram allow users to structure a story portfolio with a unique feature called **Highlights**. This is a helpful business tool).

3. **Insights**: Social media insights are statistics (data generated when users engage with your social media post/ account). These metrics produced are very helpful when trying to understand what customers think about your services.
    The amount of information accessible to you is dependent on the social media platform you are using; however, you can always make the best use of the data available to you to understand your audience better.

4. **Organic Reach**: This is the number of people who have seen your post through unpaid distribution (i.e., either because they follow your account, viewed a shared content, found you through hashtags…).

5. **Paid Reach:** Paid Reach is similar to Organic Reach; however, it differs due to the use of

paid promotional tools which helps in
boosting the visibility of a piece of content
on social media. Paid Reach usually refers to
the number of unique accounts that viewed
a post as a result of a paid promotion (Social
media advertising).

A lot of business owners try to fast-track
social media growth by spending heavily on
paid reach, but without well-structured
content, such investments will be wasted. If
your content is not appealing enough to
grow your organic reach, spending money to
promote such content might irritate your
target audience. Therefore, before promoting
your content work on them to perform well
organically.

*If your content is not appealing enough to grow
your organic reach, spending money to promote
such content might irritate your target audience.*

Facebook

Facebook is considered the largest social media platform. This fact alone makes it a go-to platform for business promotions. Here are few tips on how to grow your business using Facebook:

1. Create a **Facebook page** for your business. A Facebook page is a public profile specifically created for businesses, brands, celebrities, causes, and other organizations. Unlike personal profiles, pages do not gain "friends," but "followers" who get to view all future updates on the page. Facebook pages come with helpful business management, promotional and analytical tools which are helpful when trying to grow business online.

2. Join or create **Facebook Groups**. This is a feature that provides a community for friends and strangers who share common interests to interact in a forum. In Facebook Groups, members do not have to add each other's accounts as friends to get access to post content in the group (unlike Facebook profiles).

Groups will help you connect with total strangers who might be in need of your products or services.

3. Use **Events** and **Facebook stories**. Facebook events is a calendar feature that notifies users about upcoming events. You can add your events on your personal account or your page to gain visibility as Facebook will show your events to users near your event venue.

    Stories just as we discussed earlier can be used to share content in an interesting way to users (span of 24 hours).

4. **Run Facebook ads**. Facebook Advertisements are targeted to users based on their location, demographic, and profile information. Promoted content is displayed in user's newsfeed, stories, Facebook messenger, and even Instagram. You can maximize the effectiveness of your ads by choosing the right audience & right call-to-action (will be discussed further in CHAPTER 5).

5. **Marketplace**. This is a new feature on
    Facebook that allows users to list items for
    sales (including both images and price tags).
    The Facebook Marketplace allows users to
    find products & services listed near them. It
    is a great way to create awareness and sell
    your products & services. To find out more
    about the Facebook Marketplace, click this
    link.

Instagram

Instagram is a photo-sharing social media platform with over 100 million users (as of 2020). It is owned by the Facebook company has also been a very effective medium through which Entrepreneurs sell their products and services successfully online. By default, once an account is created on Instagram, it is categorized as a personal account. In other to gain full access to the business tools needed to monitor and run a successful Business page, you will need to convert your Instagram profile from a **personal** to a **business account** by connecting your Instagram account to a Facebook page. To find out more about how to convert your Instagram account to a business account see more details via this link.

Here is helpful guidance on how to maximize Instagram for Business:

1. Create an **appealing Bio**. A bio is a brief description of your business, website links, and call to action (email, call, message buttons). Your bio is the first thing users see when they visit your profile and needs to be carefully structured if you want to get the attention of potential customers. Through the use of Instagram Stories highlights, and **social media link referencing** landing page platforms such as LinkTree (https://linktr.ee/) and Disha (https://disha.ng/pages/), you can spice up your bio and provide very useful information to visitors (this will go a long way to increase your chances of gaining followers and even Clients).

2. Make good use of Stories and Instagram Live stream feature. Create engaging video content and upload it to Instagram **Reels, IGTV,** and stories to boost engagement.

3. It is important to boost your engagements because this is what the Instagram algorithm (just like other platforms) uses to recommend your profile to other users. This can be done by creating content that encourage your followers to **like, comment, share, tag people, send direct messages, or save**. Because people have tried to cheat the algorithm over the years through fake engagements (robot likes, comments), platforms have continuously improved their algorithms to make the best recommendations. For this reason, when trying to evaluate the importance of content on a platform like Instagram, **post saves** are ranked to have more value than likes and comments and the reason is simple. It takes a user with genuine interest to save an Instagram post, while likes and comments don't necessarily imply interest.
It is very important to understand how this works because this will help you make smarter decisions that will attract customers.

4. Use **Hashtags, tagging,** and **locations** to smartly increase your reach. These are creative ways to increase your reach organically and although they can get irritating when used poorly, they have good results. Hashtags help users interested in your post topic to find your content and that is why you need to use hashtags that actually relate to the content you created. Adding locations on the other hand helps users near you to find your content and this is very good for business. Locations can be added to both feeds and stories.
 Tagging can become irritating if not used appropriately. Tagging was designed to allow users to call the attention of other accounts to a post. When you tag accounts to Instagram accounts, the post appears under "Tagged contents" and the account gets notified.

5. Use the **Shop feature**. The shopping feature is available to Instagram Business profiles and allows shopping items to be tagged

directly to posts. Find out more about setting up the shopping catalogue via this <u>link</u>.

6. Run Instagram ads.

Twitter

Unlike Instagram and Facebook, Twitter is a microblogging system that allows you to send and receive 140 characters short posts (tweets) which can include links, photos, audio, and video. Twitter is very powerful and connects its users more than any other platforms by allowing people to share their thoughts with a big audience (without necessarily having to follow users). Twitter allows users to discover stories about trending news and events through using or trending topics and hashtags.

A lot of success stories of Entrepreneurs who got their business breakthrough on Twitter go a long way to show that Twitter is a great place to grow your business organically because the audience on Twitter is highly engaging and only the best contents thrive. Over the years Twitter has shown itself to be a powerful medium not only successful in the business space but also in political debates, protests, and cries for justice.

Twitter also allows users to run effective ad campaigns.

LinkedIn

Unlike most social networks, LinkedIn is a professional networking social media platform. LinkedIn helps professionals make business connections, share their experiences, CV, find and apply for jobs. LinkedIn keeps evolving as it also allows users to develop their skills online through tutorial courses and certification. LinkedIn has a paid subscription package called LinkedIn Premium which gives users access to helpful learning tools and insights that can help users improve and land business opportunities online.

LinkedIn also allows Entrepreneurs to manage their business online by creating **LinkedIn Company pages** (a feature similar to Facebook's page feature on Facebook). This gives the user the ability to run ads and target potential customers and investors. To find out more about how to set up your LinkedIn Company profile, visit this <u>link</u>.

WhatsApp and Telegram

WhatsApp and Telegram are both text-like mobile app social media platforms that allow users to send messages, images, audio, or video in a similar way as traditional text messaging service. Telegram has some features that make it a preferred choice for users such as support for large group size (as much as 200,000) as well as some interesting security features.

WhatsApp on the other hand has helpful features for business owners. These features include functions like broadcast messages, WhatsApp stories (status), Voice & Video conference calls. It also has a dedicated app that comes with additional business tools for Entrepreneurs called the **WhatsApp Business** app.

The WhatsApp Business app comes with some interesting features which include but are not limited to:

1. An advanced Profile
2. Catalogs
3. Quick Replies
4. Labels

Blogs and Vlogs

One of the most effective ways to build **brand awareness**, while providing relevant and useful content to your target audience is through consistent blogging. Good blogging also helps to improve your business appearance on search engines as well. I will briefly work you through some important blogging platforms.

YouTube

YouTube provides a simple way for people to store videos online and share them with others. The great thing about YouTube is that you can also earn good money when your content gets high traffic (once you sign up for AdSense).

In order to upload videos on YouTube, you will need to create a YouTube Channel. Your channel is where you group the videos you make and upload, the videos you watch and like, and the playlists of videos you create. Just like social media, you have to work creatively to improve your content engagement & one of the ways to do this is through the effective use of YouTube keywords when uploading videos. YouTube channel keywords are terms that give YouTube information and context about your channel. They help YouTube understand the type of content you produce and who your target audience is (similar to the use of Hashtags on Social media). Using keywords appropriately increases your Video post's visibility on YouTube.

WordPress

WordPress is a software that helps users to set up blog compatible websites to manage web content, allowing multiple contributors to create, edit and publish articles. This is a very useful tool when you want to setup up a customized blogging platform. To find out more about setting up a WordPress blog, visit this link.

Medium

Medium is a social publishing platform for writers and readers. Medium has a paid subscription for readers while allowing writers to join and publish for free. Medium is a good blogging choice because you would not have to build a readers list from the bottom up. Once you work on great content and have worked on your keywords appropriately,

readers will gradually be able to find your content.
To read more about how to work with Medium to
create mind-blowing articles, visit this link.

Newsletters

Email marketing has become one of the most
abused forms of marketing online. A lot of
businesses are doing it wrong by spamming mail
recipients with unwanted content. However, this
does not mean in any way that email marketing is
dead. In fact, it remains a very successful method to
communicate with an online audience if done the
right way. An Email newsletter is a type of email
that can be used to communicate the latest news,
tips, or updates about your product or company to
your audience.

Sending newsletters to users who did not subscribe
(are not interested) to you is spamming and this is
bad for business because the purpose of email
marketing is defeat when subscribers do read your
mails. Here are tips on how you can get better
results with email marketing:

1. Build a targeted subscriber list (don't spam).
    Try to collect emails by either requesting
    audience to subscribe via a website or social
    media ads. Another creative way is to use
    freebies as bait because that way you are
    sure they are interested in the type of
    content you are serving.
2. Have a clear goal and plan towards that. Do
    just send random emails, let your content
    flow in structure (don't be all about
    promotions. Care about your readers by
    providing useful content, that is how you
    will get their attention).

3. Plan creative follow-up emails. Remember
    you have a goal, so you need to follow-up
    because the chances that you will get replies
    are slim (even when the audience enjoyed
    your content).

4. Use appealing email subject lines. Your
    subject is the first thing your audience gets
    to see when they receive your email so you
    need to be creative about the message

embedded in your subject. Please note that while it is important to have to use appealing subjects, **DO NOT LIE!** Lying to lure users to read your content doesn't normally end well (instead it will trigger/irritate your audience).

5. Create a **good email design and copy** (hire a copywriter if you have to). You are talking to strangers so if your email does not attract them (visually or conversationally) they will not be patient to stick till the end of the email.

CHAPTER 4 - Building Trust

In this chapter, you will review the missing piece in your business; earning the trust of total strangers. Before we dive in, I will like you to digest this question:

Will you still deposit your money in a Bank if the news says they are going bankrupt?

Why is Trust so important?

But seriously, why Trust? Every Entrepreneur understands that to build a successful business they need:

1. A great product/ outstanding service.
2. Effective marketing strategy &
3. Great customer experience

However, Trust is that invisible but very essential factor needed for success and it becomes even more important for businesses that run online. Trust is the core of branding; if customers don't trust your brand, they would not patronize your business at all. You need to understand the role of trust when trying to build a business that sells online because more than 80% of your potential customers will be

*__More than 80%__ of your potential customers online will be people who do not know you personally and have every reason to doubt **your integrity**.*

people who do not know you personally and have every reason to doubt your integrity.

Building Trust

In general, customers have the belief that businesses are trying to fool them by charging them **outrageous prices**. Also, people are scared of

getting scammed either by receiving **substandard products/services** or by falling victims to **Internet Fraudsters**; understanding the customers' pain points will help you know how to win them over.

It is also important to note that building trust takes time. This means that you should not expect the results to be instantaneous. These are practical ways to build trust for your brand:

1. **Get your Brand licensed/Incorporated.** Registering your business enhances the reputation and perception of your business. It also makes customers more comfortable working with you. Corporate Clients (especially companies) are more comfortable hiring or engaging with registered companies.

2. **Integrity.** Be truthful when communicating with potential customers, don't be unnecessarily secretive. When you lie or hide information, you give customers room to doubt you. Always give your customers all the options available and let them choose even if it means they don't get to buy from you. Never deceive customers into buying from you.

---

*Always give your customers all the options available and let them choose even if it means they don't get to buy from you. **Never deceive customers into buying from you.***

---

3. **Make your billing as transparent as possible.** When customers know what they are paying for they will trust you and will understand your pricing better. I understand that the price of some raw materials/raw could consistently change. However, try to communicate this to your client. Also, don't

be quick to give the client a quote until you
have evaluated the cost of executing the job.
It is unprofessional to keep changing prices

---

after giving your customer an initial
quotation.

4. **Show customers that you can be trusted
    with their personal information, delivery of
    products & services.** Don't give customers a
    reason to doubt you. Invest in the structure
    of your business and this will build trust.
    If you have a website, invest in security (buy
    SSL to protect your domain), secure your
    business accounts because anyone who can
    hijack your business page automatically
    gains access to private customer details such
    as emails, phone numbers, photos, Date of
    Birth, or even credit card information. Hire

or consult a Tech Expert (it is always best to be safe than sorry).

Also, if you deliver products; try to structure your delivery so customers are confident that purchased goods will get to them in one piece.

5. **Share reviews and testimonials that provide social proof from other satisfied customers.** You can request reviews ethically from your existing customers and let potential customers see what other customers are saying about your business. It is important however that you don't fake it because if your business is not good enough to get genuine positive reviews sooner or later your new customers will see what your business is. So rather than faking reviews, work to improve your products/ services so that they get those reviews truthfully.

CHAPTER 5 - Making Sales Online

I know you have waited so long to get to this chapter because this chapter is the main business. After trying to upskill, build an online community, and build trust, you want to know how these all convert to sales.

Before we dive in, just evaluate yourself using these questions:

1. Have you purchased something from a stranger (online/ offline) before?
2. What was the most compelling factor that made you pay for that service or product?
3. If you have abandoned completing a purchase online, what made you have cold feet?
4. Do you buy from people with great products/service even when you don't like them?

I need you to understand that because we are dealing with humans, we cannot overlook the **role of emotions** in business. People buy products/ services (especially luxury items) for **the**

experience and **feelings**: the reason a businessman would buy a Ferrari is not just because he wants an automobile to solve the problem of transportation. He pays that much money because he wants to experience luxury and feel good. The same goes for a Lady with a designer product. Understanding this is crucial to the success of your business online, SELL THE EXPERIENCE & FEELING.

Identifying the right Platforms & Audience

Knowing the right platform for your business is not something you can know by using some almighty formula. It is not easy to predict if people will be interested enough to buy or not buy from you simply because of the platform you choose, however here is a guide that will get you better results. To decide the platform that is best for your audience you will need to answer these questions about your potential customer profile:

1. How old are they?
2. Are they male, female, or both?
3. What is their income and education level?

4. What are they interested in outside of your
    product and service?

For instance, LinkedIn is a platform that appeals
more to professionals. It has News, professional
resources, and article-like posts. The atmosphere
here is a lot tensed and serious in comparison to a
platform like Twitter.

If you are not so clear on which platform to work
with, feel free to experiment by trying to all-out
and observing the platform that gets the attention
and engagement. After getting engagements, try to
convert those engagements to sales.

How to find potential Clients

How do you know people who are interested in
your product/service? Every business owner needs
to know this because if you do not market smartly,
you will exhaust yourself mentally. Below are
metrics you can use to find potential customers and
what they find appealing.

1. **Mentions, Saves & Repost**. I consider this
    category as one of the effective ways to

know genuine interest. Likes are easy and don't necessarily show interest (sometimes they are more supportive than interest-driven). Whenever someone gets mentioned to your post, it is a clear sign that such a person is mostly to find the type of content you are promoting on that particular post appealing. Saves and repost work in a similar way.

2. **Comments and Likes**. Even though these are considered weaker metrics, it does not in any way mean they are ineffective. When you reach out to someone who drops a comment or likes, you stand a better chance of converting such users to paying clients.
3. **Direct Messages and Follows**. These are also strong indications that the products/ services you are selling are not appealing to the user.

Now that you know how to find social media users who are more likely to your services appealing, you need to know how to find them. Here are ways to find them:

1. Engagements from your account followers/ fan base.
2. Engagement gotten as a result of the use of Hashtags, location tags.
3. Engagements from online advertising (paid).

We will discuss how to reach out to these potential customers smartly in the incoming subsections so that they do not runoff.

Online Advertising

Before you begin running an online ads campaign, you need to define your goals clearly. These goals are what you hope to meet after the online ads are over and they could be:

1. Driving sales;
2. Sign-ups to your website/social media/channel landing page
3. Increase Video views
4. Drive post engagements

5. Alert users about discounts, and promotional events
6. Create brand awareness
7. Get Direct Messages from potential clients
8. Get users to download App/E-book/resources
9. Etc.

When you have a clear advertising goal, you will be able to choose an effective call to action. A Call to Action is typically a button or a link. It is used (on a social media post) to tell the user exactly what action to take and how to take it (e.g., **Subscribe, Send WhatsApp message, Download App, Watch Video, Call, Visit Website, Book Now**, etc.). Choosing the right CTA helps to boost your chances of converting a user into paying clients. To learn more about how to use call-to-actions click this link.

Converting engagements to Sales

This is the point a lot of business owners get wrong. I strongly recommend you as a business owner not to allow the strong want to sell to make you spam your potential customers. This will only drive them away.

Allow them to get familiar and a little comfortable with you before try pitching. I am sure you will also not take a spammed message/ email seriously. In the next section, we will be discussing the right way to handle DM Marketing (email marketing can also adapt this strategy).

DM Marketing: the right way

DM Marketing simply means sending private messages to potential customers in an attempt to try to convert them to paying clients. Let's go straight to business and see how to do it the right way, let us discuss the **DOs** & DON'T of DM marketing.

1. **Minimize Automated & Generalized messages**. Whether you are sending a WhatsApp/ Twitter message or an email, try to take your time to personalize your messages. The recipient should feel that you thought about them. Sending generic messages is annoying and will irritate the client and then convert them to paying clients.

2. **Research and Identify Your Target**. Know a little about them (not creepy stuff), but at least go through their profile and try to understand them.

3. **Try to build Relationships**. I know you want to sell to them, but don't act too selfish. Many business owners run away when they get a NO, that is not good business. Build a relationship and be genuinely interested in helping the person, so that you don't have to walk away or be disrespectful if the user declines your offer.

4. **Don't be fake or too patronizing.** People can sense a fake show of affection, so be natural. Remember you are messaging

people who have been assessed potential buyers, so do not repel them by being fake (be yourself).

5. **Be conversational.** Do not just send paragraphs without giving the recipient the chance to respond. Most users won't even respond and will automatically classify your message as spam. Try to start by greeting and welcoming the users and find a common ground, then allow them to respond before you go ahead. Always try to get their reaction so that you confirm that you are on the same page.

6. **Be suggestive, do not pressure the recipient.** You might not win all your potential clients on your very first interaction, so do not be tempted into pressuring them to decide immediately. As much as you try to convince them, allow them to build trust in your brand.

There are many ways to begin a DM Marketing conversation. As you practice and study your prospect carefully you will find smarter and more ways to connect with them. However, I have attached a screenshot sample of a DM Marketing conversation.

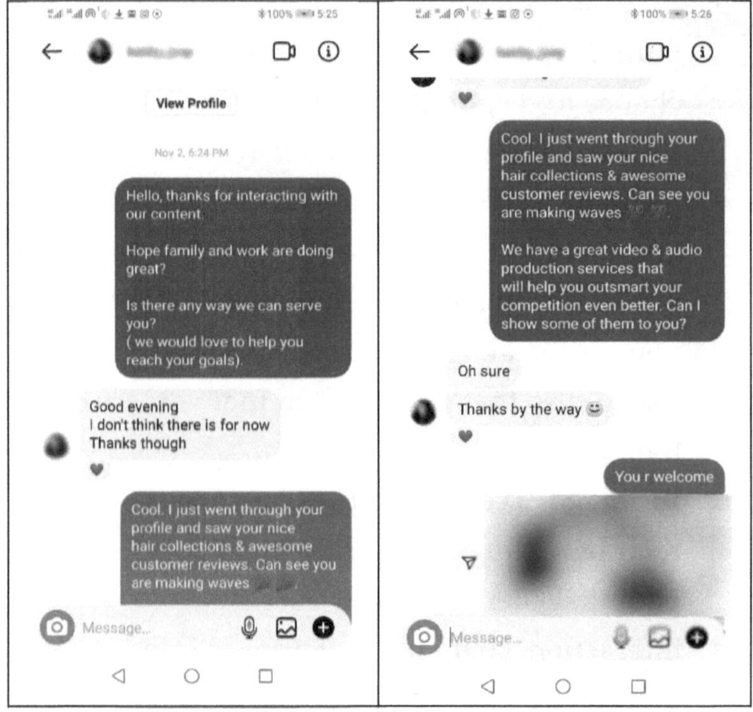

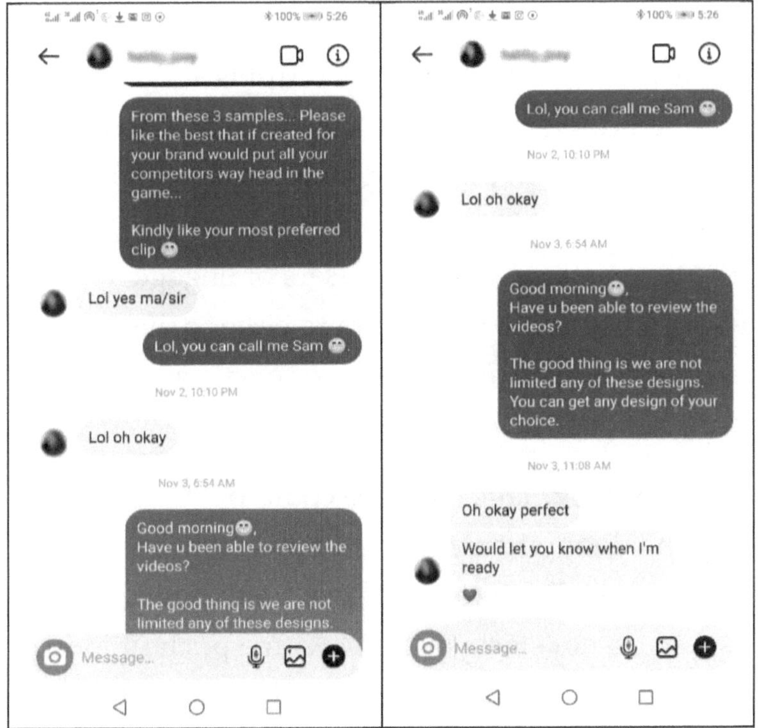

From the conversation above, it is clear that the ice was broken & although the recipient did not make an immediate purchase, chances are that they will after they have developed trust in the brand.

Guidelines to create a Great Sales script

What is a Sales Script? A sales script is a
prescribed conversation framework created to help
business owners to pitch and close deals with
potential clients. You can customize your scripts to;
start conversations with new users or engage
existing followers with the aim to either drive sales,
offer freebies/discount/promos, or create awareness
about your product/services.

1. **Greeting.** This message could open or shut
    the door when you send messages to a new
    contact. Remember they do not know you,
    so do not start your DM with a pitch (it most
    times does not end well). Allow the potential
    client to get comfortable, **greet and wait for
    a response.** You need to find out what are
    your potential customer needs by asking
    him/her. Here is a sample script:

    *Hey **[Client first name]**! Thanks for interacting
    with my content. Looks you have great taste in
    quality shoes. I'm **[Your name]**, the CEO of
    [Business name]. My passion is making jewelry*

from beads. Is there any way I can help you today?

The normal response will be a **NO** so you have to plan a response (do not insist if you do not receive a friendly response).

2. **Offer.** Use your discretion to have a friendly conversation with the prospect (however be natural, do not be fake).
    Most business owners will run after a No. however you can follow-up with a question like:

    Alright. We recently launched a new shoe collection for men. Looking at your profile, I think you would love these designs. Can I share a few designs with you? Hope you don't mind?

    If the client says No, respect their decision. Do not pressure them. However, if you are given the go-ahead, select a few designs and ask the client to select their favorite design.

Now at this point, you have begun, to interact with the potential customer. This is the point where the potential customer might request for price or tell you they are not ready. This is the moment to tell them why your services and products are the standards and why they should consider doing business with you.
Do not pressure the potential customer to buy on the spot. Allow them to ask questions, think about it, allow them to vet you.

3. **Objections.** 'I am not ready for this', "I will think about it', 'it is too expensive', 'I don't need this', etc. These are common responses you should anticipate and have answers for. Never allow yourself to get irritated when you are trying to pitch to a client & remember, not everybody will buy immediately from you when you pitch and that is okay. Your response will go a long

way in winning over some people with
doubts (in the long run).

4. **Closing.** These are the messages with which
   you will close the purchase. Always
   appreciate people who respond to your DM
   messages (whether they show interest in
   your offerings or not).

There is no such thing as a Failed Ads

I intentionally, used a chat that did not
immediately convert to a sale to prove one point;
just because they did not buy immediately does not
mean the marketing failed.

This is the philosophy I work with. I believe and
want to work with this belief, that when you
promote/ pitch your product to a new potential
customer there are three possible outcomes:

1. They are so interested in your product; **they
   buy**.
2. They are skeptical about your
   brand/product; **your brand just gained
   more awareness**.

3. They hated your brand; **will never buy from you**.

Most times we however see it from only 2 angles instead of 3. Not everyone who didn't buy hates your brand. Most of these prospects are just skeptical, so instead of feeling discouraged, work to win their trust.

CHAPTER 6 - Online Business Laws & Guides

You need to be aware of business laws and guidelines if you are choosing to run your business online. Educating yourself will save you a lot of trouble. These guides and laws fall into the following category.

General best practices online

These are guidelines every Entrepreneur must know because they cover basic business ethics such as Trademarks, patents, and copyrights.

For instance, if you sell branded t-shirts with popular logos on them (without due permission), you might run into trouble if the brands pick offense.

Region/ Location specific rules

When you decide to go international, you need to be aware of the business laws guiding the region you want to step into. Some countries have shipping restrictions on specific products (*Alcoholic beverages, Ammunition, Animals, Explosives, Fresh fruits and vegetables, Hazardous materials, and so on*) while others have regulations on personal data (for software solutions). For instance, the General Data Protection Regulation (GDPR), which went into effect 25 May 2018, creates consistent data protection rules across Europe and applies to all companies that process personal data about people in the EU, regardless of where the company is based.

You also need to learn about the tax laws because various states and countries have different expectations and standards when it comes to taxes. Do not begin operating ignorantly as it might hurt your business in the long run. Speak to a Tax professional to gain more insight on this subject.

Product-specific guides

Depending on the product or service you are offering, you need to research if there are restrictions that affect the product you are selling to in the region you are targeting. For instance, there are books, apps, and products that have age restrictions, it is important to abide by these restrictions when advertising online to avoid penalties and unnecessary complications.

Platform-specific guidelines

Whether you are trying to use social media platforms or blogging platforms, you need to beware of the terms and conditions stated on the respective platforms. Most of these companies have guidelines that describe the type of content, practices, and advertising strategies allowed on the platforms. For instance, Facebook has an ads policy that does not all promotion of posts that contents direct or indirect assertions or implications about a person's race, ethnic origin, religion, beliefs, age, sexual orientation or practices, gender identity, disability, medical condition (including physical or mental health), financial status, voting status, membership in a trade union, criminal record, or name.

Find out more about Advertising policies for various platforms:

- <u>Facebook</u>
- <u>Twitter</u>
- <u>LinkedIn</u>
- <u>Google</u>

CHAPTER 7 - Securing your Business & Customers against Fraudsters

Have you ever been scammed? It is definitely not a pleasant experience. Unfortunately, many of us act carelessly until we get into trouble. Prevention is said to always be better than cure. You don't have to wait for your business accounts to be hijacked before your take precautionary measures.

A shocking stats by <u>Security Boulevard</u> shows that 85% of all organizations (in the USA) have been hit by a phishing attack at least once and 95% of all attacks targeting enterprise networks are caused by successful **phishing** (precisely spear phishing). This shows how important it is for you as a business owner to protect your business against phishing attacks.

How does Phishing work

Phishing (also called social engineering) is a type of cyber-attack often used to steal user data (*login credentials and credit card numbers*). It usually happens when the attacker/ Scammer poses to be a legitimate organization and dupes an unsuspecting victim to open an email/ text message with malicious content/link, instant message, or give sensitive information via call.

While Phishing strategies keep changing, there and a couple of patterns that can be used to find phishing attacks. Some of the patterns you should watch out for include:

1. Suspicious messages that contain offers that are too good to be true.

2. The unusual sender or unusual tone from a familiar sender (could be a sign of a hijacked account).

3. Unnecessary sense of urgency to take action on suspicious content.

4. Links from strange senders or suspicious attachments especially .exe files.

Social Media

As a business owner selling online, you need to secure your business accounts across all platforms because any successful hijack by scammers will hurt your business and customers. **Please secure your accounts!!!**

One of the best ways to secure your accounts (asides from choosing a strong password & logging in on only Trusted devices) is to activate Two Factor authentication on all your social media accounts.

Two-factor authentication is a method used into login to an online account or computer system which requires the user to provide two different types of information. With two-factor authentication, you'll need to first provide **a password** (accurate password of course) and prove your identity some other way to gain access (usually using SMS code verification). To learn how to activate your two-factor authentication, watch this tutorial videos:

1. Facebook- Watch Video.
2. Instagram- Watch Video.
3. Twitter- Watch Video.
4. WhatsApp- Watch Video.
5. LinkedIn- Watch Video.

BONUS CHAPTER: Some Helpful software tools for Business owners

Due to limited operating budgets and small staffs, most business owners spend a lot of money or time trying to handle day-to-day tasks with little to no time for long-term goals & strategic planning. In this chapter, I put together a short little of helpful tools that will have you save time and resources, letting hire experienced hands only when it is necessary.

Accounting & Finance

1. QuickBooks (https://quickbooks.intuit.com/)
   Description: Accounting software package that can be used for invoicing customers, paying bills, generating reports, and preparing taxes.
   Operating System: PC & Mobile
   Subscription type: Free trial & Premium

2. Invoice Bookipi (https://www.bookipi.com/)
   Description: A cloud-based invoice maker app that sends professional invoices and estimates to customers.
   Operating System: PC & Mobile
   Subscription type: Free

3. Wave App (https://www.waveapps.com/)
   Description: It is also invoicing & accounting software with credit card processing & payroll services useful for income, tax, and expense tracking.
   Operating System: PC & Mobile
   Subscription type: Free

4. Invoice Simple (https://app.invoicesimple.com/)
   Description: An invoice platform that allows users to send professional invoices and receive payments from customers.
   Operating System: PC & Mobile
   Subscription type: Free & Premium

Project Management

1. Trello (https://trello.com/)

   Description: It is a collaboration tool (project management tool) for projects.

   Operating System: PC & Mobile

   Subscription type: Free & Premium

Digital writing & Editing

1. Grammarly (https://www.grammarly.com)

   Description: Grammarly helps users to create error-free text content in Gmail, Facebook, Twitter, LinkedIn, and any other app you use. It scans text for common grammatical mistakes (like misused commas) and complex ones (like misplaced modifiers).

   Operating System: PC & Mobile

   Subscription type: Free & Premium

Video Editing

1. Quik - (Android & [IOS](IOS))

   Description: The Quik app, allows users to create awesome videos with just a few taps.

It works with Templates and automatically syncs the video to the selected soundtrack.
Operating System: Mobile
Subscription type: Free & Premium

2. Filmora (https://www.wondershare.com/)
Description: It is a software that allows users to edit videos, splice together multiple videos, and leverage effects like overlays and other video editing features.
Operating System: PC & Mobile
Subscription type: Free & Premium

Flyer Editing

1. Canva (https://www.canva.com/)
Description: Canva is a graphic design platform, used to create social media graphics, presentations, posters, documents, and other visual content.
Operating System: PC
Subscription type: Free & Premium

2. Coolor (https://coolors.co/)

Description: Coolors is a color palette app and website that allows users to create beautiful color schemes for their graphic designs and brands.
Operating System: PC & IOS
Subscription type: Free & Premium

3. Remove bg (https://www.remove.bg/)
   Description: This is an online platform that removes the backgrounds 100% automatically in images that contain people.
   Operating System: PC
   Subscription type: Free & Premium

4. Pexels (https://www.pexels.com/)
   Description: Pexels is a free stock photo and video website and app that helps designers, bloggers, and everyone who is looking for visuals to find great photos and videos that can be downloaded and used for free.
   Operating System: PC
   Subscription type: Free

5. Unsplash (https://www.unsplash.com)

Description: Unsplash is a free stock photo website and app that helps users find great photos that can be downloaded and used for free.

Operating System: PC

Subscription type: Free

Video Conferencing

1. Zoom (https://zoom.us/)

    Description: Zoom is a cloud-based video communications app that allows you to set up virtual video and audio conferencing, webinars, live chats and screen sharing.

    Operating System: PC & Mobile

    Subscription type: Free & Premium

2. Stream Yard (https://streamyard.com/)

    Description: Stream Yard is also a cloud-based video communications app that allows you to set up virtual video and audio conferencing, webinars, live chats and screen sharing.

    Operating System: PC (Browser)

Subscription type: Free & Premium

3. Jitsi (https://jitsi.org/)
    Description: Is an open source cloud-based
    video communications app that allows you
    to set up virtual video and audio
    conferencing, webinars, live chats and screen
    sharing.
    Operating System: PC & Mobile
    Subscription type: Free

Email Marketing

1. Send in Blue (https://www.sendinblue.com/)
    Description: It is an email and messenger
    marketing platform that was built for
    sending emails, creating forms, SMS creating
    chatbots and automated workflows.
    Operating System: PC (Browser)
    Subscription type: Free & Premium

2. Flodesk (https://www.flodesk.com/)
    Description: It is an Emailing platform that
    allows users to design and send on-brand

marketing emails, create opt-in forms to
grow your list, and build email automations.
Operating System: PC & Mobile
Subscription type: Free trial & Premium

3. Mail Chimp (https://mailchimp.com/)
   Description: It is an email marketing
   platform that helps users manage and send
   mails to clients/ subscribers.
   Operating System: PC
   Subscription type: Free & Premium

Payment Gateways

1. Stripe (https://stripe.com/)
   Description: It is a software that allows
   business owners to integrate and accept
   payments and manage their businesses
   online.
   Operating System: PC
   Subscription type: Processing fee of 2.9%

2. Selar (https://selar.co)

   Description: It is a Nigerian ecommerce tool
   creatives & entrepreneurs use to sell their
   content, products & services across borders.
   Operating System: PC
   Subscription type: Processing fee of 4% +
   NGN 50

3. Pay Stack (https://paystack.com/)

   Description: It is a Nigerian-based software
   that allows business owners to integrate and
   accept payments and manage their
   businesses online.
   Operating System: PC
   Subscription type: Processing fee:
   - 1.5% + NGN 100 (Local)
   - 3.9% + NGN 100 (International)

4. Flutterwave (https://flutterwave.com)

   Description: It is a Nigerian-based software
   that allows business owners to integrate and
   accept payments and manage their
   businesses online.
   Operating System: PC

Subscription type: Processing fee:

- 1.5% (Local)
- 3.8% (International)

Social Media

1. Link Tree (https://linktr.ee/)
   Description: It is a link-in-bio tool that allows users to create a landing page and structuring multiple links to content.
   Operating System: PC
   Subscription type: Free and Premium

2. Disha Pages (https://disha.ng/pages/)
   Description: It is also a link-in-bio tool that allows users to create a landing page and structuring multiple links to content.
   Operating System: PC
   Subscription type: Free and Premium

3. Buffer (https://buffer.com/)
   Description: It is a software application for the web and mobile, designed to manage

accounts in social networks, by providing the means for a user to schedule posts to Twitter, Facebook, Instagram, Instagram Stories, Pinterest, and LinkedIn.

Operating System: PC

Subscription type: Free and Premium

Samuel N. Theophilus

Samuel "Nnitiwe" Theophilus is a Computer Scientist with a skill set in Software Development, Graphic Design, IT Consultation, Digital Marketing, and Writing. He hails from Tula in Kaltungo LGA, Gombe state in Nigeria. Samuel graduated with First class degree in Computer Science from Bingham University and was also received the award for the best graduating student in the faculty of Science and Technology in 2017.

He is the Co-founder of Nnitiwe Tech Limited and has been its CEO for over 4 years since its inception. Over the years, Samuel has gained experience in helping Entrepreneurs to put their businesses online through active project execution, Coaching & Training sessions with Business Coaches such as Steve Harris.

Keep in touch with Samuel via the web:

Site: https://nnitiwe.disha.page/

Facebook: https://www.facebook.com/nnitiwe

Twitter: http://www.twitter.com/nnitiwe

Instagram: https://instagram.com/nnitiwe

LinkedIn:
https://www.linkedin.com/in/samuelnnitiwetheophilus

Email: *nnitiwe@gmail.com*

Company: Nnitiwe Tech Ltd

Nnitiwe Tech Limited was founded in April 2016 when Samuel Theophilus and Samuel Jabani came together with the dream of building a firm that would not only offer high-quality services, but also one that would become the source of mind-blowing innovation and transformation.

The Company was incorporated on the 5th of December,2017 by CAC with the RC 1456657.

Currently, Nnitiwe Tech helps Business Owners to Build, Grow, Promote & Attract customers with a powerful Web reputation and online advertising. The Company's services include but is not limited to:

1. **Software development** (Websites, Mobile Apps)
2. **Visual, Marketing & Publication Design** (Logo Design, Book Covers, Powerpoint Slides, Flyers, etc.)
3. **Motion graphics** (Logo reveals, Explainer Videos, 2D/3D Animation)

4. **Voice Over** (Explainer, Promotional
    Content)
5. **Online Ads (**Google, Social Media Ads).
6. **IT Consultation**.

Reach out to Nnitiwe Tech Limited using any of
the channels listed below.

Company Website: https://www.nnitiwetech.com/

Facebook: https://www.facebook.com/nnitiwetech

Twitter: https://www.twitter.com/nnitiwetechNG

Instagram: https://instagram.com/nnitiwetech

LinkedIn:
https://www.linkedin.com/company/nnitiwetech/

Email: *nnitiwetech@gmail.com*

www.ingramcontent.com/pod-product-compliance
Lightning Source LLC
Chambersburg PA
CBHW031213160726
47992CB00006B/2716